For Lisa Hunt and Karen Zuegner,
dear friends and fellow artists,
in appreciation and inspiration.

Goddess
INSPIRATION
ORACLE GUIDE

written and illustrated by

Kris Waldherr

LLEWELLYN PUBLICATIONS

WOODBURY, MINNESOTA

FIRST EDITION
Second Printing, 2007

The excerpt from *The Odyssey* by Homer on page 2
was adapted from a translation by Samuel Butler, 1900.

Llewellyn is a registered trademark of Llewellyn Worldwide, Ltd.

ISBN: 978-0-7387-1167-6
This book is a component of the *Goddess Inspiration Oracle* kit,
which consists of a boxed set of 80 full-color cards,
a tarot bag, and this perfect-bound book.

Visit the *Goddess Inspiration Oracle* online at www.goddessinspiration.net.

Llewellyn Publications
A Division of Llewellyn Worldwide, Ltd.
2143 Woodale Drive, Dept. 978-0-7387-1167-6
Woodbury, MN 55125-2989, U.S.A.

www.llewellyn.com
Printed in the United States of America

Table of Contents

PART THREE:
ADDITIONAL INFORMATION

Part One

"Still Odysseus kept grieving about not being in his own country, and wandered up and down by the shore of the sea bewailing his hard fate. Then Athena came up to him disguised as a young shepherd of delicate and princely mien, with a good cloak folded double about her shoulders . . . Odysseus was glad when he saw her, and went straight up to her."

—*THE ODYSSEY*, HOMER

*I*nspiration. The word itself is expansive. It brings to mind the invigorating intake of air into lungs, filling us with energy. It suggests a world charmed with possibilities, unfolding in a sudden flash of light. Haven't we all heard someone say, "I had no idea what to do next. Then, out of the blue, I had an inspiration. It was like magic."

Where did that inspiration come from? What made it take form?

The word *inspiration* itself suggests the mode of its creation. Its first syllable, *in*, means to create inclusion, to set limits to that which is limitless. It forces something shapeless to take shape—similar to what happens when water is contained within a cup, or air inside a balloon. Its second syllable, *spir*, is taken from the word *spiritus*, the Latin word for breath—meaning to breathe life into something in order to animate it, to fill it with spirit.

Inspiration. To take spirit into ourselves. Like the air surrounding us, we cannot see inspiration. But it is there nonetheless. And it animates us when we least expect it.

When most people think of inspiration, they usually connect it to the mysterious activities of artists and poets. Though inspiration is primarily associated with creative endeavors, it is much more than that. It opens us to possibilities beyond what our rational mind can perceive. In some cases, it takes the form of intuition, an internal knowledge that often keeps us safe and protected. But most of all, inspiration allows us to practice an invaluable skill I call "flexible thinking."

Flexible thinking is the ability to think outside the box, so we may find a solution to a dilemma when there appears to be none. It is nonlinear in form, arriving in flashes of images and ideas instead of neatly packaged within an obvious answer that can be deduced empirically. Flexible thinking allows us to be receptive to possibilities, to listen before we act. It encourages us to bend like a willow tree in the wind instead of shattering into pieces when confronted by adversity.

If we use the standard wisdom that the feminine represents the receptive principle (or yin) and the masculine is active (or yang), then flexible thinking is feminine in nature—divinely feminine, if you will. The same equation can be written of inspiration itself.

As representatives of the Divine Feminine, goddesses have been honored through the ages for their capacity to encourage inspiration. In ancient

Greece, the Muses were praised for their ability to breathe life into scholarly and artistic works. The Celtic goddess Brigit was invoked for the spark of creativity. Her sacred holiday of Imbolg, celebrated every February first, included rituals designed to increase creativity. The Oracle of Erda, the Norse goddess of the earth, invited mortals to find inspiration within nature's blueprint; divine will could be discerned by watching the patterns of waves or the movement of clouds across the sky.

These are only three examples in which goddesses provide us with the inspiration we need to transform our lives. Within the *Goddess Inspiration Oracle* you will find an additional seventy-seven—a total of eighty deities who represent essential aspects of the Divine Feminine.

About the Divine Feminine and Goddesses

The *Goddess Inspiration Oracle* presents the wisdom of the Divine Feminine in a manner meant to spark inspiration in you. But what exactly *is* the Divine Feminine, which some also call the Sacred Feminine?

In recent years, the Divine Feminine has gained much attention due to the blockbuster success of *The Da Vinci Code*. Because of this phenomenon, some might consider the Divine Feminine tangential only to Mary Magdalene and a suppressed history of women in Christianity. But the Divine Feminine encompasses more than Mary Magdalene, as overlooked as she has been. It expands to embrace the innate wisdom and strength so many women possess in abundance, the very spirit which animates us.

As I have noted in previous books, one way in which the Divine Feminine has been honored over the ages was in the form of goddesses—women of sacred and eternal power. As such, these divine women represented the concerns of the people who worshiped them. The goddesses were invoked to provide a generous harvest, a safe birth, a happy afterlife, and much more. In other words, they held dominion over all aspects of life and death.

Some believe that many of these goddesses originated from a supreme triple goddess. Similar in structure to the Christian trinity of father, son, and holy spirit, but older in origin, the triple goddess traditionally reflected the three stages of a woman's life: maiden, mother, and crone. Each of these goddesses corresponded to the phases of the moon, with the waxing moon representing the maiden, the full moon the mother or fertile woman, and finally, the waning dark moon the crone or post-menstrual woman.

As humans became more sophisticated in their spiritual and emotional needs, it is thought that the triple goddess became splintered into innumerable deities. Individually, these goddesses serve to represent different aspects of life. Combined, they comprise the complex and all-encompassing force of the Divine Feminine.

Just as goddesses have been present throughout history, I firmly believe that inspiration is always present in the world. As an artist and author, I experience this all the time—even the genesis for this deck came in a sudden flash of inspiration when I least expected it! However, sometimes inspiration may not be as accessible as we wish. During these fallow periods, tools such as the *Goddess Inspiration Oracle* can help us become receptive to the knowledge we most need at that moment.

About Oracles

Oracles bear the double duty of being both the message as well as the vehicle in which to communicate this message.

In the ancient world, the term *oracle* referred to the sacred place where prophecy was received as well as the person channeling it. One famous example is the Oracle of Delphi, located on Mount Parnassus in the heart of the Greek empire. It was sacred to the deities Apollo and Gaia and served by numerous priestesses known as the Pythia. Pilgrims would travel far distances to consult the Oracle of Delphi, granting great import to the communications offered there. An article in *National Geographic* magazine in 2001 suggested that the Pythia's messages were encouraged by ethylene—a gas with narcotic properties—escaping from the earth itself. Presumably it enabled the priestesses to bypass their conscious minds in order to receive the messages needed from the other side.

Today, many consider an oracle the message itself; to quote media critic Marshall McLuhan, the medium is now the message. The knowledge granted by the oracle offers necessary information from a new source, hopefully bypassing human fallibility. The oracle may be predictive in nature, or it may simply provide us with an objective mirror in which to observe a situation.

Whichever definition you prefer, the function of an oracle remains the same: oracles offer information. How we choose to interpret this information and what we decide to do with it is up to us. They often provide us with an experience of synchronicity, a term created by the Swiss psychologist Carl Jung to describe a series of seemingly random events that connect within us to gain a deeper meaning.

In the case of an oracle, our personal experiences synchronistically connect with it, thus creating a message unique to our situation. By doing so, the oracle helps us release information we already possess deep within our psyche. It frees us to see with new eyes.

About the Goddess Inspiration Oracle

From time immemorial, oracles have been used to gain inspiration from the goddess. It is my fervent hope that the *Goddess Inspiration Oracle* continues in this tradition.

To create the *Goddess Inspiration Oracle*, I took inspiration from the more than one hundred goddesses I have described in art and words during much of my professional life. From these, I chose eighty goddesses who represented a wide variety of women's concerns. As I worked, inspiring messages organically emerged from their stories and my paintings. These messages offer creative solutions, comforting reassurances, and, most importantly, a new point of view to consider. They are intended to act as a catalyst for change.

Though I had previously created a deck devoted to the Divine Feminine—*The Goddess Tarot*—the *Goddess Inspiration Oracle* is intended to offer this wisdom to all women, not just to those who work with tarot. It presents a portrait of the Divine Feminine that expands beyond the wonderfully rich archetypes of the tarot.

I believe that we are surrounded by divine inspiration, that it often appears in mundane forms in our everyday life to tell us what we need to hear. People of ancient times also believed this. The Oracle of Erda, which I described earlier, reminds us that the natural world can provide us with sacred messages from the goddess.

Another beautiful example of goddess inspiration is described in Homer's *Odyssey*. Throughout Odysseus's long journey home from the Trojan War to his wife, Penelope, the goddess Athena mysteriously appears incognito to help the warrior when he is most in need. Sometimes the goddess disguises herself as his trusted friend Mentor; other times she takes on the form of a stranger who happens to be at the right place at the right time. As such, the goddess grants Odysseus and his allies the exact information they need to know at that moment, without disclosing her divine stature.

These types of fortuitous interactions happen more often than we realize. We receive the divine inspiration we need to transform our lives but simply don't recognize it in its disguised form. In a novel or film, such convenient coincidences might be belittled as examples of *deus ex machina*, god—or goddess—in the machine; and they are, in the best possible sense of the expression.

The *Goddess Inspiration Oracle* was created to help you become more receptive to these experiences, and, by becoming more receptive, to encourage them. It is intended as an instrument for inviting the inspiration of the Divine Feminine into our lives when we most need it.

We are meant to be filled with joyful inspiration, to spill over with exuberant spirit. May the *Goddess Inspiration Oracle* animate your life with inspiration, providing you with an intimate experience of the Divine Feminine.

The structure of the *Goddess Inspiration Oracle* is intentionally simple. It is intended to be accessible to everyone, whether you've previously read about goddesses or have no prior knowledge. Unlike a tarot deck, there are no special systems to learn or card meanings to memorize. You can use the *Goddess Inspiration Oracle* right out of the box—everything is provided within this deck and book. The only thing required is your receptive spirit.

The *Goddess Inspiration Oracle* deck is comprised of eighty alphabetically arranged cards. Each card features a portrait of a goddess and a brief description of the attribute by which she is honored in her native culture. Included is a message inspired by each goddess and her story.

These messages can also be used as an affirmation. Affirmations are valuable tools that enable us to rewire our personal expectations. Instructions on how to do so are presented later in this section.

This book expands upon the cards by offering additional information and keywords for each goddess. These descriptions are intended to help you identify and connect with their particular energy.

The goddesses presented in the *Goddess Inspiration Oracle* are drawn from traditions and cultures around the globe. They range from popular goddesses (such as Venus, the Roman goddess of love) to lesser-known ones who deserve greater acknowledgement (such as Ogboinba, the Nigerian goddess of prophecy). These deities represent a wide sample of the Divine Feminine in her many forms and functions.

There is a tendency among some who work with goddesses to judge these divine women as being either light or dark of quality. The term "light" usually connotes a fortuitous goddess such as Lakshmi, the Hindu goddess of prosperity; "dark" suggests an intense goddess such as Pele, the tempestuous Hawaiian fire goddess. This type of thinking divides deities into good and bad, positive and negative, black and white. It ultimately limits our experience of the sacred.

While some of these goddesses may initially seem intimidating in their power, they all offer positive, nurturing inspiration. If you do experience trepidation upon encountering a particular deity in the *Goddess Inspiration Oracle*, it might be worth examining whether there's something she reminds you of that needs acknowledgement or a preconception that requires release. We often project onto others things that discomfort us in ourselves. By recognizing when this occurs, we can free ourselves.

Additional information about each of the goddesses featured in the *Goddess Inspiration Oracle* can be found in the expanded tenth anniversary edition of *The Book of Goddesses,* as well as in publications by myself and other authors. A selected bibliography is included at the end of this book.

Working with the Goddess Inspiration Oracle

The best way to begin working with the *Goddess Inspiration Oracle* is to familiarize yourself with the goddess cards before reading this book's text descriptions. This will help you create a more direct relationship with the cards and their art.

Begin by taking conscious possession of your cards. You can create a ritual to invest them with your energy, such as smudging them with sage or visualizing white light around them. You can also say a simple prayer for inspiration, such as this one, excerpted from the Beauty Chant of the Navajo people:

> *In beauty may I walk.*
> *In beauty may I see.*
> *In beauty may we all be.*

However you choose to proceed, it is important that you invest your cards with your very best intentions. Ask them to offer you only positive, healing information and inspiration. Find a special place to store your cards where they won't be handled casually by others.

Next, allow yourself to look through the cards. As you handle each one, you are also imbuing your energy within them. Take note of what emotions, if any, you experience as you consider each card—these provide information to be considered. Are there particular goddesses you feel drawn to? Which of their messages ring true to your condition? Conversely, did you have a negative or apathetic reaction to any of the goddesses? If so, do you know why?

If you like, you can write these thoughts in a journal. Use them as a starting point for automatic writing. See where your words take you—you might visit some unexpected places! To free your inhibitions, you can even ask the goddesses for answers and imagine their responses.

If you haven't used this creative tool before, automatic writing is a popular exercise used by writers to jump-start inspiration. It helps to break down barriers between the conscious and unconscious mind. To begin, set an egg timer to five minutes, then put pen to paper and write. Allow your hand to lead you, not your brain. If you find yourself judging or censoring your efforts, *don't*. I know that this is easier said than done, but automatic writing is about freedom, not criticism. When the egg timer rings, stop writing, even if you're in the middle of a sentence.

If you find yourself becoming too self-conscious with your words, try using the opposite hand than you usually write with. For example, if you're left-handed, try writing with your right. Sometimes this can trick the dominant side of our brain into losing inhibitions.

Once you have processed the cards and considered any writing you might have done, move on to reading this book's individual goddess descriptions. Note the keywords associated with each goddess. Again, see what attractions or reactions that arise as you read about each goddess.

Please feel free to use these text descriptions as a starting point for your own associations. This allows you to personalize the *Goddess Inspiration Oracle* for yourself, creating your own experience of synchronicity.

Card Readings

The simplest way to work with the *Goddess Inspiration Oracle* is to choose a card at random.

First, take a moment to center yourself—a moment's meditation or lighting a candle can prepare a properly receptive mood. Then formulate your question for the oracle. The proper phrasing of a question helps to improve the quality of the answer. Words reveal our intentions: a query such as "What do I need to know at this time?" usually elicits a more helpful answer than a question requiring a yes or no answer. Composing the question also helps to compose your mind so that you will be more receptive to the inspiration offered.

When you are ready, shuffle the deck a random number of times. Cut the deck, and take the card at the top. Alternately, you can also place the cards face down in a pile and allow your hand to be guided. When your fingers touch the "right" card, you will know it. Occasionally when you are shuffling, a card will fall from the deck onto your lap. This card can also be consulted for guidance.

After you choose your goddess card, you can consult this book for further information. As described earlier, take note of any personal reactions or emotions you might experience as you consider your card. This allows you to personalize your oracle reading to your experiences. As well, brainstorming can often invite connections that might be initially inaccessible. For example, the veil over Fortuna's eyes could remind you of a game of hide-and-seek from your childhood; the demeanor of another goddess might resemble a friend you need to reach out to.

The *Goddess Inspiration Oracle* can also be used in card spreads, such as those utilized for a tarot deck. A useful spread for many situations is the past-present-future spread. To begin, choose at random four cards. Then place as so:

The first card represents the past; the second card, the present; the third card suggests a possible future. A final card offers a summary of the situation being examined. Additional card spreads can be found in many books about tarot or online.

While most people are eager to use oracle decks to obtain guidance, even more are interested in predicting the future. My personal belief is that the future is always fluid. While an oracle can reveal what the future might hold, our actions in the present continuously affect it. Therefore, if you receive an answer from the *Goddess Inspiration Oracle* that discourages you, find a way to affect change: choose action in the present.

In other words, take responsibility for your future by being responsible. Consider your predictive readings a reflection of the moment, if things continue as they have been. They suggest what we need to do, not what will actually happen.

Though self-empowerment is the primary intention for the *Goddess Inspiration Oracle*, you can use the cards to inspire others. Reading for others requires responsibility, however, and should be undertaken with only the highest respect for the querent. Remember, your words have authority.

Creative Work

The *Goddess Inspiration Oracle* is especially intended to be used in conjunction with creative work. Whether goddesses are creating the world or creating peace, they provide us with inspiring examples of creativity that we can use as role models for ourselves.

If you are feeling stuck while working on a creative project, you can ask the oracle, "How should I next proceed?" Then choose a card. Use this goddess message as a call to action. Even if you change your mind later on, at least it got you moving!

Affirmations

Affirmations offer a direct way to put the Divine Feminine into action. They allow us to change negative thought patterns, thus freeing us to create a new road map for our lives. Affirmations also empower us to be self-sufficient—since we are giving ourselves positive feedback, we are not so reliant on others for praise.

To create an affirmation using any of the cards from the *Goddess Inspiration Oracle*, simply change the message written upon them into a first-person statement. Since words are a powerful tool for intention, this trains our subconscious into accepting the statement as fact.

For example, for Athena, the message on her card is: *Be independent. Listen to the wisdom within yourself.* To create an affirmation, you would change the message as so: *I am independent. I listen to the wisdom within myself.*

Try stating your affirmation whenever you need strength or sense a loss of focus. Alternately, you can write your affirmation when you wake each morning and before you go to sleep. At these times, our minds are often more receptive to suggestion.

Part Two

The Goddess Cards

Abeona

EXPANSION

PROTECTION

LEAVE-TAKINGS

Originally worshiped in ancient Rome as the goddess of departures, Abeona protected children as they left their home to enter the great world. She watched over them as they took their first steps, helping them guide one foot in front of the other. In this way, a child is able to explore wider realms: a hallway leads to a room; a room to a gateway; a gateway to the outside world.

In the eyes of the universe, we all are children. Whenever we start something new, it is as if we are learning to walk for the first time. We may stumble initially. But if we persist, we will discover new vistas beyond what we originally expected.

Beyond your home is a world to be discovered.

Explore it.

Aditi

MOTHER SPACE

CREATION

UNIVERSE

NURTURANCE

In India, Aditi is honored as the creator of life. For it was Aditi who gave birth to the gods and goddesses; they, in turn, brought everything into consciousness, thus creating what we consider reality.

This benign goddess is addressed as Mother Space because she gave birth to the planets and stars. Some associate her with the endless sky; appropriately, her name translates as "limitless."

Her children, known collectively as the Adityas, are connected with the twelve months of the year. They also symbolize the twelve signs of the zodiac, whom some believe control fate.

Your thoughts create reality.
Be conscious of what you choose.

Aine

LOVE

LIGHT

MAGIC

The Irish goddess of love and light, Aine was honored on midsummer night. Associated with both the sun and the moon, Aine's popularity is proven by the shrines devoted to her throughout the Celtic world. Some believe that during the Middle Ages, the influence of Christianity discouraged worship of Aine. Even so, her powers could not go unacknowledged: Aine, goddess of light, was transmogrified into a *leannan sidhe*, a magical fairy queen whose powers could be used for mischief.

Stories abound of Aine, the fairy queen. One warned that a romantic dalliance with Aine led to an ecstatic death—a folktale probably encouraged by Christian monks to encourage monogamy. Another tale honors her as the mother of the fairies through her encounters with mortal men. As such, she suggests the power of love to spread magic in the world.

Magic is afoot. Find a way to encourage it.

Ajysit

GODDESS OF BIRTH

FATE

SOULS

BIRTHING

The goddess Ajysit, worshiped by the Yakut in Siberia, was believed to materialize during the birth of a child. This deity functioned as both midwife and spiritual mother. During the birth, Ajysit used her powers to relieve the mother's labor pains. After the birth, the goddess took responsibility for the new baby's soul. Some believed that Ajysit possessed a book of fate, almost like a registry for each soul issued at birth.

The story of Ajysit serves as a beautiful reminder that each of us possesses a soul with a unique blueprint; this blueprint maps out the bountiful gifts we can offer the world. Sometimes we require help to give birth to these talents lying dormant within ourselves. A midwife such as Ajysit can ease our labor pains as we do so.

Look for help to appear when you most need it.

Amaterasu

EXPANSION

LIGHT

REFLECTION

A benevolent solar goddess, Amaterasu is the supreme deity of Shintoism, a religion practiced primarily in Japan. Upon her birth, her parents were stunned by how brilliantly Amaterasu shined with light. They asked her to climb the celestial ladder to heaven and illuminate the world.

A famous myth concerns Amaterasu's anger with her brother, the storm god Susanoo. He was so noisy with his destruction that she chose to withdraw from the world. The goddess hid herself in a cave, thus plunging the earth into darkness. But balance was restored when Amaterasu was lured out by laughter and entranced by her reflection in a mirror. To this day, shrines to Amaterasu use mirrors as symbols of her brilliance.

You are meant to shine.

Go out into the world and reflect light.

Annapurna

NOURISHMENT

GENEROSITY

HARVEST

Many Hindus believe that Annapurna helps create food to nourish the world. Often honored at harvest festivals, this generous goddess is depicted in beautiful statues and paintings as sitting upon a grand throne, offering food to a small child. As an avatar, or incarnation, of the mother goddess Durga, Annapurna represents the bounty that the world seeks to offer us.

Sometimes when a delectable meal is offered, we distrust the bounty spread before us; this meal can take the form of actual food or something else that nurtures our spirit. Instead of enjoying it, we put ourselves on a diet of self-righteousness. The universe is eternally bountiful—take advantage of what is offered you.

A harvest awaits you. Enjoy it.

THE EMBRACER

WATER
PROSPERITY
FERTILITY

In ancient Egypt, the goddess Anuket was acknowledged as the benevolent giver of life. She was primarily associated with the nurturing waters of the Nile. Some considered her the actual incarnation of the Nile, with its two tributaries symbolizing her arms. Appropriately, Anuket's name translates as "the embracer." It also suggests the way the waters of the Nile embrace the fertile banks surrounding it.

Anuket was honored during the annual flooding of the Nile with an ecstatic festival of thanks. During it, her devotees would throw offerings of gold and other precious objects into the river, which would be swept away in the rapids. One can imagine how happy those who lived downstream would be to discover these riches on their shores.

Your life will overflow with blessings.

Astarte

ETERNITY

STARS

SEXUALITY

This Assyrian goddess is one of the most ancient deities honored by humanity—her shrines date from the Neolithic period of the Stone Age. Honored as the Queen of Heaven, Astarte was thought to rule over stars, who were believed to be the brightly shining spirits of the dead. This connection to death also suggests another function of Astarte as a goddess of war.

However, most consider Astarte an early incarnation of Aphrodite, the Greek fertility goddess whose Roman counterpart is Venus. As such, Astarte is associated with sexuality and love. One of the symbols for Astarte is a circle surrounding a star, representing the planet Venus.

Use the past as a lesson.
Move forward with love.

Athena

BRILLIANCE

REASON

INDEPENDENCE

The daughter of the Greek god Zeus and his first wife Metis, whose name means "wisdom," Athena was born under unusual circumstances. She emerged from her father's head fully clothed and fully armored after Zeus split his head with an axe to relieve a headache.

Athena chose to devote herself to wisdom and art, thus avoiding the romantic intrigues of the gods and goddesses. The goddess's primary physical attribute are her bright grey eyes, which suggest her clarity of purpose. Though many associate Athena with war, she often used reason over force to outwit her enemies. She is also noted for her skill as an artisan.

Just as Athena was incubated within Zeus's head, we all hold wisdom in our brains. Her story encourages us to think independently.

Be independent. Listen to the wisdom within yourself.

Baba Yaga

LIFE CYCLE

STRENGTH

OLD AGE

Many of us recognize Baba Yaga as an evil, child-eating witch with a home set upon chicken claws, which is how she is presented in Russian fairy tales. Originally this goddess represented the life cycle, from birth to death. In Hungarian folklore, she was acknowledged as a good fairy.

The word *baba* means old woman; the chicken claws bear the wrinkled appearance of aged hands. This imagery suggests the fear that some might feel upon seeing an extremely elderly woman—it's not surprising that in many fairy tales, the witch is an old hag. However, if we are wise enough to bypass appearances, we can see the beauty within.

Do not fear life's changes,
no matter how scary they seem.

Bastet

HAPPINESS

FERTILITY

LOVE

In ancient Egypt, the cat was worshiped as the sacred animal of Bastet, the Egyptian goddess of happiness, love, pregnancy, and birth. Bastet is usually depicted with the head of a cat and holding an ankh, a symbol of fertility and eternal life. Records from this period tell us that Bastet's temples were home to hundreds of cats, which were cared for by her followers.

Because cats are incredibly fertile and affectionate, devoted mothers, Bastet was considered to have many of these same happy qualities as her feline devotees. Their playful qualities allow them to find happiness in unexpected ways: a cloud of dust becomes a toy; a feather transforms into a mouse to bat about. They invite us to find joy in unexpected ways.

Allow yourself to be as lighthearted as a cat.

Benzai-ten

GODDESS OF TALENTS

WEALTH

HAPPINESS

ARTISTRY

Happiness can come from wisdom as well as beauty, music, and art. The Japanese goddess Benzai-ten is the goddess of all these inspiring gifts. She is believed to bring happiness and wealth—appropriately, the middle syllable of her name, *zai*, means "talent" or "wealth" in Japanese. Sometimes the goddess is portrayed with eight arms bearing open hands, symbolizing her many talents and all-encompassing generosity.

Benzai-ten's realm lies beneath the beautiful waters of Lake Biwa, where she is believed to be married to a dragon king; the goddess was able to tame him through her love. Water is a universal symbol for wealth, usually of the financial kind. To be able to share one's talents with the world in exchange for personal wealth is the happiest of situations.

Your talents can bring you wealth. Look for opportunities.

Berchta

FATE

THE HOME

WINTER

The German goddess Berchta was associated with the art of transforming flax into linen, symbolizing her ability to spin the thread of destiny. She also presided over other household affairs traditionally associated with women. During medieval times, she was considered a witch by Christians suspicious of the old ways.

Perhaps because the turn of a spinning wheel suggests the turn of the seasons, Berchta was believed to wear a mantle of snow upon her shoulders. Some said the goddess appeared to her followers as a young woman, while others claimed she took on the form of a white-tressed crone. This suggests Berchta's ability to embody both past and future within herself.

The seeds of the future already lie within you.
Find serenity as it unfolds.

Brigit

THE FIERY ARROW

POETRY

ARTISTRY

FIRE

The fire of inspiration is a gift many yearn to experience. Celtic people of long ago entreated the goddess Brigit for this divine spark. In Scotland, Brigit was seen in the form of a beautiful white swan, as elusive as inspiration itself. She was also called the Fiery Arrow because she was associated with the art of smelting, which uses the alchemical tool of fire to transform base metals into valuable objects.

Brigit's sacred holiday, the feast of Imbolg, is observed the first of February. To receive her wisdom, many would hang a white wool cloth outside on the eve of Imbolg. The next morning, they fetched the cloth, believing it had absorbed the energy of the goddess. This sanctified cloth would be set aside in a special place, to be called into service when inspiration was required from Brigit, goddess of creativity.

Be ready to burn with inspiration.

Changing Woman

TRANSFORMATION

THE EARTH

NOURISHMENT

Changing Woman, also known as Estsanatlehi, is one of the most powerful deities of the Navajo Holy People. A benevolent fertility goddess, she is most often associated with corn, the grain that so many cultures rely upon for nourishment. Changing Woman symbolizes the ever-changing and ever-fertile earth. As suggested by her name, she appears as a young maiden for the spring and summer and transforms into an old woman for the fall and winter.

The teachings of Changing Woman are presented within the Blessingway, a group of essential rituals and chants. The songs and ceremonies that make up the Blessingway are used throughout the year for weddings, childbirth rites, coming of age, and other occasions in the life of the Navajo.

All of life's seasons bring blessings. Appreciate them.

Chang O

QUEEN OF THE MOON

WOMEN

FAMILY

CYCLES

Around the world, the moon is associated with numerous objects. The fanciful believe it is made of cheese because of its pocked surface. Others claim to see the face of a man in the moon. In China, the moon is associated with a celestial white rabbit, who is said to reside there with the goddess Chang O in a palace built of fragrant cinnamon wood.

Every September, when the full moon is at its most brilliant, the Chinese honor Chang O with a moon festival. This celebration also celebrates women and features family reunions. Besides gathering to admire the moon's luminescent brilliance, people bake special round treats called moon cakes, which are filled with delicious red bean paste. As people eat them, they are reminded of Chang O, queen of the moon.

Celebrate your femininity with pride.

Cimidye

SUFFERING

TRANSCENDENCE

TRANSFORMATION

The story of Cimidye, a Tucuna Indian goddess of the Amazon, presents us with an example of vengeance and transcendence. After Cimidye was abandoned by her cruel husband in a deep forest, she encountered a spirit guide in the form of a large blue butterfly. The butterfly took pity upon her and magically transformed the girl into a dragonfly. In time, they were able to take revenge upon her husband, thus freeing Cimidye from her marital vows.

Dragonflies are potent symbols of illusion and impermanence. In Zuni mythology, they are shamanic creatures who act as intermediaries between the spirit and physical world.

Your difficulties transform you.
Take heart, for you will be vindicated.

Cybele

THE EARTH

CATHARSIS

REBIRTH

In Phrygia, now part of modern Turkey, Cybele was honored as the great mother goddess. She was associated with caves and mountains and with the Greek earth goddesses Rhea and Gaia. Each spring, Cybele was worshiped in wild, ecstatic rites that commemorated the death and rebirth of her son-consort, the vegetation god Attis. These emotionally intense ceremonies offered her followers a sense of catharsis and suggest her connection to the fertile soil.

Since she reigned over beasts, Cybele was also honored with the title of Mistress of Animals. She was traditionally represented with lions, who were often depicted drawing her chariot, and bees. As well, her consort Attis was associated with bulls, which were sacrificed in his behalf.

Acknowledge your animal nature.

Danu

WISDOM

PROSPERITY

LEADERSHIP

Danu was honored in ancient Ireland as the greatest and wisest of all Celtic goddesses. She is considered to be the mother of the deities known collectively as the Tuatha Dé Danann, whose name translates as "the people of the goddess Danu."

A benign deity, Danu is believed to provide her followers with prosperity and knowledge. She is associated with the rivers, whose flowing waters suggest the abundance brought by this goddess. Some even consider the Danube, which runs through much of Europe, to bear her name; this suggests the expansive reach of Danu, goddess of knowledge.

Use your knowledge to prosper. You have the tools.

Demeter

THE SEASONS

MOTHERHOOD

LOSS

Demeter, Greek goddess of the harvest, is considered the mother arche-type of the triple goddess. Her story has offered consolation through the ages to mothers everywhere and serves to explain the seasons.

When Demeter's daughter Persephone was abducted by Pluto, god of the underworld, to become his bride, she searched to the ends of the earth for her child. Demeter soon learned that Zeus had allowed Pluto to wed Persephone. At this news, grief and fury overwhelmed the goddess. So that the earth might reflect her sorrow, Demeter halted all plants from flowering and ripening, thus creating winter for the first time.

The main ritual associated with Demeter was the Thesmophoria, which allowed women to work though pain. It allowed them to honor their grief and recognize its goddesslike divinity.

Honor the divinity of your grief. Then spring will return.

Diana

WOMEN

THE MOON

STRENGTH

Diana, the Roman goddess of hunting and the moon, reveals the physical strength and self-reliance of women everywhere. She was praised for her strength and athletic grace; her skill as a huntress was unsurpassed. Independent and wild, Diana chose to join her life with no man. Instead, she lived unencumbered in the woods, her only companions a loyal band of nymphs and untamed animals.

Diana was associated with the moon, which rules over the night, wild beasts and women's bodies. She was usually depicted wearing a lunar-shaped crown upon her brow. Many of the goddess's rituals encouraged girls and women to join together and dance wildly in the light of the full moon, thus expressing their strength and athleticism.

It is time to hunt for what brings you strength.

Erda

WISDOM

FATE

DIVINATION

The Norse earth goddess, Erda, lived in a cave within the earth's deepest recesses, which was set next to the roots of Yggdrasil, the vast world tree. Yggdrasil was watered by Erda's plentiful fountain of wisdom. Erda's powers were as encompassing as Yggdrasil's leafy span—the goddess and her magical fountain were often invoked by those in need of her far-reaching wisdom. Others believed Erda could bend the inexorable powers of fate over which she ruled.

Because of Erda's association with fate, the Norse thought there was a clear correlation between the goddess and the art of divination. They often turned to the earth itself for guidance, using many aspects of it as oracles—animals, birds, the sky, even the ocean. They believed observation of these phenomena could offer divine answers.

Look to the earth for answers.

Erzulie

SENSUALITY

LOVE

WEALTH

This Voodun goddess is known for the luxury that she delights in—silken clothing, rich jewelry, and fragrant flowers. Not surprisingly, Erzulie usually appears to her followers beautifully dressed and perfumed.

Also a goddess of love, Erzulie wears three wedding rings upon her hand; these bands represent her three husbands, the sky deity Dumballah, the ruler of the sea Agwe, and Ogoun, the warrior hero. She is noted for her girlish, flirtatious manner.

Erzulie's traditional symbol is the heart, which suggests the expanse of her domain. She is also associated with the moon, the heavenly body associated with the home and the world of the emotions.

Use luxury to soften your heart.

Fortuna

SURPRISE

LUCK

CHANGES

Initially considered a fertility deity, the goddess Fortuna reigned over the laws of chance. Fortuna was honored throughout the Roman Empire in numerous incarnations, all made specific to the supplicant's needs. For example, newly married women honored Fortuna as the goddess Fortuna Virginensis. They offered her the garments from their bridal night so that she might smile upon their unions.

Generally considered benign of favor, Fortuna was later viewed as unpredictable in her inclinations. In medieval manuscript paintings, Fortuna is traditionally depicted blindfolded, suggesting the arbitrary and sometimes surprising nature of chance. She was also shown with two faces, one smiling and the other bearing a frown.

Believe in your good fortune.

Freyja

LOVE

BEAUTY

ART

The Norse goddess Freyja presided over the living and the dead. As such, she was responsible for the souls of half the warriors who perished in battle. Despite this grim duty, Freyja was mainly honored as a goddess of beauty and love—forces more powerful than war and death—no doubt because of her exquisite beauty. Sometimes she rode through the sky in her golden chariot drawn by two grey cats. At other times, she wore a falcon-skin cloak, which enabled her to fly through the air like a bird.

When compared to the pragmatic needs of life, beauty is something society often views as unnecessary. But it is a nurturing force that all humans need—how empty our lives would be without beauty! Beauty offers us an authentic experience of the divine that can shake us to our core. The story of the goddess Freyja reminds us of its healing power.

Acknowledge the power of beauty.

Fricka

DESTINY

MARRIAGE

MOTHERHOOD

Also known as Frigga, this ruling goddess was married to Odin, the most dominant god of the Norse pantheon. Fricka's vast domains encompassed love, marriage, motherhood, and destiny. She is known for her talents as a spinner of gold threads, which some believe symbolized the creation of sunlight. It also suggests Fricka's ability to spin the future; in ancient times, many thought that the art of weaving imitated the creation of fate.

In the *Prose Edda*, a collection of myths from thirteenth-century Iceland, Fricka was acknowledged as "foremost among the goddesses."

You can be foremost among women.

Take aim to reach your goals.

Gaia

CREATION

THE EARTH

CONNECTION

In ancient Greece, the earth was personified as a mysterious goddess called Gaia. A cosmic, procreative womb who emerged out of the primeval void called Chaos, it was believed Gaia existed before all other life. She was also credited with creating life. Though Gaia was powerful unto herself, she did not choose a solitary existence. The goddess formed from her womb the sea, which she called Pontus, and the sky, which she called Uranus. She took Uranus as her husband. Sky lying upon earth created numerous children within the goddess's great womb.

The myth of Gaia reminds us of the interconnection of the world—and the importance of living in harmony with its resources, as well as our fellow humans.

You can create your life.
Envision what you desire it to be.

Glispa

GODDESS OF HEALING

HEALTH

MUSIC

SHAMANISM

The Navajo of the southwestern United States pay homage to this mysterious goddess, who brought them the Beauty Chant. Glispa taught them the ways of music and healing, imbuing them with the power of shamans.

Though music brings pleasure, it is also a healing force—its powerful vibrations and rhythms realign our spirits. Drumming especially can create a doorway to the spirit world and is used by shamans around the globe. In Siberia, the shaman would straddle his drum and beat it as if it were a steed transporting him to the realm of the spirits. Native American traditions enlist drums and chants as a means to create a heightened state of consciousness. The vocalization of tones in chants can also bring forth a state of healing.

Healing powers lie within you.
Use music to access them.

Gwenhywfar

FIRST LADY OF WALES

LEADERSHIP

WISDOM

WATER

In Wales, white-water waves are called "the sheep of the Mermaid." That mermaid is the goddess Gwenhywfar, who was honored as the first lady of the Welsh islands and sea. Some identify Gwenhywfar as the daughter of the first Welsh bard, the giant Ogyrvan. In Germany, she is called Cunneware, which means "female wisdom." But today most people recognize Gwenhywfar as Queen Guinevere, the unhappy consort of King Arthur.

Since Gwenhywfar symbolized the throne of Wales, no king was able to rule without her by his side. It is little wonder that many would-be kings attempted to abduct her. They did not understand that it was Gwenhywfar's power that made them sovereign, not some forced romantic involvement. Many of these myths worked their way into Arthurian legend.

You are a wise ruler of your realm.

Haltia

STRUCTURE

LUCK

DOMESTIC AFFAIRS

Haltia was believed to rule over houses among the Baltic Finns. This benevolent goddess was considered an integral part of the actual structure of the home, bringing good luck to its inhabitants. She also acted as a guardian to the occupants of the house she had chosen to bless.

In later years, Haltia's powers were dispersed, perhaps due to the influence of Christianity. The name "Haltia" came to connote a group of male and female fairies concerned with domestic affairs, rather than a single majestic goddess.

Encourage harmony in your home.
Then good luck will visit.

Hathor

THE GOLDEN ONE

PROSPERITY

LOVE

FERTILITY

Hathor was honored in ancient Egypt as the Golden One—a divinity powerful enough to help with dilemmas ranging from love difficulties to the lack of prosperity. A goddess of fertility and plenty, she was believed to be mother to the pantheon of Egyptian gods and goddesses. Many also identify this goddess with the Milky Way, that beautiful band of stars so visible on dark, moonless nights. Appropriately, Hathor was also honored as the Mistress of Heaven. She was so popular that at one point she was served by sixty one priestesses in her temple.

From the earliest times, Hathor was petitioned for assistance in creating personal abundance, such as help with a love affair. Rituals also invoked the goddess for communal abundance, as in the creation of a generous harvest to feed everyone.

Prosperity awaits you. Look for examples of it in action.

Haumea

BIRTH

FERTILITY

VEGETATION

Haumea, a Polynesian goddess, was credited with teaching women how to give birth by pushing their babies out from between their legs. Before this, folklore claims that children were cut from their wombs, extracted by knife like a pit from ripe fruit. Thanks to Haumea, women were able to forego this dangerous passage.

Another myth claims that the goddess Pele was born from the goddess's armpit. This suggests the overwhelming fertility of Haumea—life was created from all of her body, not just her womb. Haumea was also credited with giving birth to many fantastic creatures who populated the earth. Also a goddess of vegetation, Haumea is honored as the mother of Hawaii. It is appropriate that a goddess so closely associated with fertility would be tied to this verdant island paradise.

You will safely give birth to something powerful.

Hekate

THE DARK ONE

MENOPAUSE

WISDOM

THE SUPERNATURAL

In ancient Greece, Hekate was honored as the Dark One, a mysterious goddess who brought knowledge from the realm beyond life. As the wise crone aspect of the triple goddess, Hekate symbolizes the dark or waning moon—the time when the moon withholds its light before it illuminates the night sky once more.

During these times, women who had reached menopause were believed to hold their life-giving powers within themselves, like the dark moon. They were thought to be empowered by their retained womb blood. Like Hekate, they were crones, crowned with the intelligence of their years.

As goddess of the dark moon, Hekate was also affiliated with storms, howling dogs, and willow trees. She is symbolized by a golden key, able to unlock untold riches from heaven and earth.

Gather wisdom from deep sources.

⌒ 53 ⌒

Heqet

FERTILITY
FROGS
WATER

The Egyptian goddess Heqet was considered the benign embodiment of fertility itself. As such, she was closely associated with the Nile River, whose waters help to nurture crops planted along its fertile banks. Heqet is usually represented with the head of a frog because the banks of the Nile are overrun with millions of these amphibians after it floods. She was also honored as the goddess of childbirth; not surprisingly, her priestesses were also trained as midwives.

Though fertility is usually associated with the physical manifestation of life, it is more than that—it is life itself. Fertility surrounds us, offering us inspiration and energy. The goddess Heqet suggests the proliferation of this expansive force.

Fertility surrounds you in numerous forms.

Open your eyes.

Hera

RELATIONSHIPS

DIGNITY

SOVEREIGNTY

Hera was honored as the goddess of marriage in ancient Greece. As ruler of this sacred institution, she was responsible for its protection. Her anger when the bonds of matrimony were not respected is perhaps as legendary as her difficult, tempestuous relationship with her husband, Zeus. Hera's wedding to Zeus was celebrated in Boeotia with a ritual utilizing symbols of the god and goddess. A piece of wood was carried to a shed in a cart drawn by oxen and set on fire. Oxen and trees were sacred to Hera; Zeus ruled over fire and lightning.

In many ways, this ancient ritual is tainted with traditional expectations of marriage. The male energy, symbolized by fire, devours the passive feminine. Happily, marital relationships have changed over time to reflect a more equitable relationship between husbands and wives.

You can invite respectful relationships.

Hsi Wang Mu

GODDESS OF ETERNITY

ETERNAL LIFE

FRUITFULNESS

FEMININITY

The people of China honor Hsi Wang Mu as the goddess of eternal life. Hsi Wang Mu lives in a golden palace on Jade Mountain, in a land called Kun-lun. Red phoenixes and white cranes, two birds that symbolize long life, are believed to keep the goddess company.

Though also noted for her beauty and grace, Hsi Wang Mu is known for her peaches—magical fruits that grant immortality to those who taste them. It takes three thousand years for the peach trees in Hsi Wang Mu's enchanted orchard to come to fruit. During all this time, the goddess patiently tends them like a mother caring for her children.

Peaches are potent symbols of feminine power and sexuality. The sensual curves within their soft, dimpled flesh are evocative of a woman's form and suggest the eternal fruitfulness of the universe.

Find what is eternal within yourself.

Huchi-Fuchi

GODDESS OF THE HEARTH

FIRE

FOOD

HOME

In Japan, Huchi-Fuchi is the goddess of the hearth. She was believed to have been honored among the Ainu, a hunting-gathering people indigenous to Japan. Huchi-Fuchi's nurturing fire is responsible for the creation of food and the warming of the home.

Some consider the name of Mount Fuji to be derived from this goddess's name, suggesting the volcanic origins of this famously beautiful mountain. Mount Fuji has long been a site for religious pilgrims who yearn to encounter its sacred energy.

Surround yourself with warmth
by creating an environment that nurtures others.

Hygeia

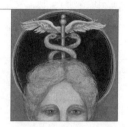

RENEWAL

HEALING

PREVENTION

The goddess of health in ancient Crete, Hygeia was identified by a serpent. The serpent is a traditional symbol of renewal, representing the cycle of disease and healing. It is also associated with Hygeia's father, Asclepius, the god of healing. Hygeia was primarily concerned with cleanliness and the prevention of illness; the word "hygienic" takes its root from her name.

The myth of Hygeia suggests that the best way to avoid disease is to prevent it. So often humans ignore their physical needs: not enough sleep, unhealthy food, lack of exercise. Disease—literally, dis-*ease* with our bodies—is often encouraged from a lack of care for them. The goddess Hygeia invites us to respect our physical needs now to avoid sickness in the future.

Healing lies in prevention. Treat your body with respect.

Iduna

KEEPER OF THE APPLES

IMMORTALITY

YOUTH

BEAUTY

The goddess Iduna was renowned for her youthful beauty and was married to Bragi, the handsome god of poetry. She was responsible for growing the golden apples of immortality in her enchanted western garden named Appleland; in the stories of King Arthur, Appleland was called Avalon—the idyllic country of immortal life. As keeper of the golden apples, the goddess was responsible for the well-being of the Norse pantheon.

The Norse people considered apples essential for the continuation of life. Associated with the resurrection, containers of these sacred fruit were placed in graves, perhaps to nurture mortals as they journeyed from one life to the next. The Norse also believed that a soul could be passed from body to body, contained within the flesh of an apple. This suggests the way that we share inspiration—by sharing the fruits of our labors.

Grow a garden and share the fruits.

Inanna

QUEEN MOON

THE HEAVENS
STRENGTH
RESURRECTION

Inanna, the great goddess of the Bronze Age, was honored as the Queen of Heaven. Some believed she was clothed with the stars. Her name translates as "Queen Moon"; the story of her descent and return from the underworld explains her connection to that celestial body.

Inanna's sister, Ereshkigal, was the goddess of death. One day, Inanna descended to the land of the dead to visit her sister. But instead of showing her hospitality, Ereshkigal killed her sister and hung her corpse on a stake. While Inanna was trapped beneath the earth, the moon disappeared from the night sky; all things ceased to grow. After three days, the water god obtained access to Inanna's corpse. He sprinkled it with the water of life, resurrecting Inanna, and she returned to the upper world, bringing the moon and all of life back with her.

If you descend into darkness, you can emerge unscathed.

Isamba

GODDESS OF THE NIGHT

THE MOON
DEATH
CYCLES

Isamba, a goddess of the Issansu people of Tanzania, was considered the personification of the moon at night. She was married to the sun god. When Isamba competed with her husband to discover which of them was the wisest, she accidentally became the creator of death. Since then, she has been associated with the cycle of life.

The moon, with its predictable cycles of waxing and waning, has long been associated with the cycle of life and death. Our individual lives also go through cycles of waxing and waning, though they may not be as clearly delineated as those of the moon. If we understand that what is empty will eventually become full again, it becomes easier to accept that all is as it should be in our lives.

You are where you are meant to be. Cultivate acceptance.

Isis

HEALING

MAGIC

POWER

Isis was worshiped in Egypt as the great mother goddess of the universe. Her name translates as "she of the throne," suggesting sovereignty. So great were her powers that only Isis knew the secret name of Ra, the sun god.

The love of Isis for her husband, Osiris, was as boundless as the jealousy of Set for his brother, Osiris. Overcome by envy, Set killed Osiris, cut his body into fourteen pieces, and scattered them over the earth. But grief-stricken Isis searched for him. When she had located every piece of her beloved, she brought him back to life for one last act of love, thus conceiving a child of him, the falcon-headed god Horus.

The powerful story of Isis continues to offer strength to women who are heartbroken from the loss of their beloved. It shows how we can create hope out of loss, like Isis's mystical resurrection of Osiris.

Your heart will be healed. Have faith.

Juno

PROTECTION

MOTHERHOOD

MARRIAGE

The ancient Romans honored a supreme goddess they called Juno. Juno ruled over all aspects of Roman life with her consort, the god Jupiter. Besides being worshiped as the great mother, this goddess was also invoked as Optima Maximus, meaning "best and greatest" of the goddesses.

Juno was believed to watch over all women from their first to last breath. It is for this reason that Roman women called their souls *juno*, in honor of the goddess. As the patroness of marriage, Juno restored peace between couples; one of her temples was used as a sanctuary for women who needed shelter from cruel husbands. To this day, many people consider the month of June, named after the goddess, to be the most favorable time to marry. The peacock is associated with Juno because the many eyes in its feathers are like the goddess's ever-open eyes as she protects women.

You are watched over at all times.

Kali Ma

THE DARK MOTHER

DESTRUCTION

CONSTRUCTION

RENEWAL

Kali Ma, a powerful Hindu goddess, is widely worshiped in India. She is considered the personification of time, which destroys everything. Though often feared, Kali Ma is necessary to life. Acceptance of Kali Ma recognizes that life cannot exist without death; death affords an opportunity for new growth to rise from the old. The goddess is often invoked for protection against disease and other destructive phenomena.

Kali Ma is terrifying of appearance. She is black of form and wears a necklace of human skulls and a belt of human arms. Her frightening presentation suggests the fears humans displace onto others when they resist change. When embraced, Kali offers the opportunity for great expansion.

Allow the old to pass. Something better awaits.

Kishijoten

PROTECTION

BEAUTY

THE ARTS

In Japan, the goddess Kishijoten is acknowledged as a protector of children. Mothers ceremonially invoke her to watch over their infants and keep misfortune away. She is also associated with the arts and beauty. Some believe Kishijoten also protects geishas, since these gifted women practice arts valued by her.

The graceful attributes of Kishijoten stand in stark contrast to those of her brother, Bishamon, the god of war. It is understandable how the desire for protection would arise when confronted by the violence of battle. Kishijoten offers us hope that those we love most are watched over by divine forces.

Those you love most are divinely protected.

Kuan Yin

MOTHER OF MERCY

COMPASSION

HEALING

SERENITY

Kuan Yin is one of the most beloved deities of China and is considered to act as a guardian angel to humans. She is said to personify *karuna*, the principle of boundless compassion and kindness. Mother of mercy, mother of compassion and healing—all these honorifics describe Kuan Yin. Today this treasured goddess is widely worshiped by Taoists and Buddhists. She is believed to heal those sick in heart and body. She pays special attention to mothers and children in distress, and even seafarers in storms.

Many people believe that even to say the goddess's name will bring protection and relief to those in need of her help. Others choose to go on pilgrimages to the goddess's temple on the mountain of Miao Feng Shan, which is set upon a faraway island. As they pray, they shake rattles and other noisemakers to attract the notice of Kuan Yin.

Become a channel for compassion.

Lakshmi

WEALTH

BEAUTY

LUCK

Lakshmi is treasured in India as the goddess of wealth and beauty. It is believed that all who look upon Lakshmi know instant happiness. She is usually depicted with her consort Vishnu, the conqueror of darkness.

Creating prosperity can be as creative an act as any artistic endeavor. Lakshmi, the goddess of abundance, shows us that wealth can be divinely inspired. As the sacred manifestation of all forms of prosperity, she is perhaps the most popular of the Hindu gods and goddesses. Lakshmi's form is often depicted upon coins as bright as the fortune she offers her devotees.

Lakshmi is believed to be attracted to sparkling jewels, which are like the riches she bestows. Statues of the goddess show her wearing gold and other precious gems and surrounded by verdant lotuses.

Welcome wealth in all its forms.

Lalita

THE AMOROUS

LOVE

FLIRTING

THE UNIVERSE

Lalita is honored in India as the goddess of love and passion. Appropriately, this deity's name translates as "the amorous." Some believe that Lalita amuses herself by playing with the universe like a flirtatious woman enticing an enthralled lover. As she does so, she creates and embodies all of life, just as the act of love can create life.

In the tantric tradition, Lalita is presented as a brilliant triple goddess with far-reaching powers of creation. She serves in counterpoint to Kali Ma, whose destructive powers encourage new life.

Love is a playful act to take joy in.

RENEWAL

SPRING

MAGIC

The name of Maia, the Greek goddess of spring and rebirth, means "the maker." Every spring this goddess is believed to make the grass and flowers grow again. She is also praised as the grandmother of magic because her son, the god Hermes, discovered that mysterious art.

Shy Maia was said to live alone in a cave on Mount Cyllene in Arcadia. Though she led a humble life, she did not escape notice: the god Zeus observed Maia's extraordinary beauty and came to her one night. From this nocturnal encounter, Maia conceived Hermes. As soon as he was born, Maia immediately knew her son was a genius. While still a baby, Hermes created the first lyre by stretching strings across a tortoise shell and the first panpipe from marsh reeds. Besides being the first magician, Hermes is credited with the invention of medicine, astrology, and letters.

To bloom, find a way to embrace the magic around you.

Maman Brigitte

GODDESS OF CEMETERIES

DEATH

RESURRECTION

CROSSING OVER

Besides being associated with death, Maman Brigitte is the goddess of cemeteries. An imposing, intense woman, the goddess often appears to her followers accompanied by a black rooster. She is thought to be fond of hot peppers and drum music. When Maman Brigitte honors the living with her presence, some claim she temporarily takes over their body to communicate with them—a phenomenon known as spirit possession. Those who are visited in this manner are considered to be blessed by her.

It is believed that Maman Brigitte protects those whose graves have been memorialized by a cross; these crosses enable the dead to enter the country of resurrection.

That which appears dead will be resurrected.
Look for it.

Mama Quilla

MOTHER MOON

TIME

MOTHERHOOD

MARRIAGE

Besides being a goddess of marriage, Mama Quilla was an Incan moon divinity—her name translates literally as "Mother Moon." One story claims that this goddess was the mother of the sun god, Manco Capac, who was also considered the first Incan. Appropriately, Mama Quilla was associated with calendars, which document the passage of time delineated by the moon and sun.

The Incan people thought that Mama Quilla was embodied in the preeminent wife of the chief. As such, this mortal woman served to represent the divine powers of the moon on earth.

Just as the moon changes over time,
so will your situation.

◎ 71 ◎

The Moirae

DESTINY

CYCLE OF LIFE

TIME

In ancient Greece, the Moirae were commonly known as the three Fates. As such, they were considered the spinners of destiny. The first Moirae was Clotho, who was believed to spin the thread of life. The second was Lachesis, who decided how much time each human was allotted. Finally, Atropos cut the thread when it was time.

The Moirae were responsible for the creation, preservation, and destruction of life, much like other triple goddesses honored around the world. So great were their powers that they were feared by both humans and the immortals of Olympus.

Trust in the fate before you.

The Muses

GODDESSES OF INSPIRATION

THE ARTS

SCIENCE

CREATIVITY

Invoked by poets, artists, and musicians, these nine nymphlike goddesses presided over the arts and sciences in the world of the ancient Greeks. The Muses offered their supplicants the purest form of inspiration—literally infusing spirit into creative works to animate them.

Though their parentage is uncertain, most stories hold that the Muses were the daughters of Mnemosyne, the goddess of memory, and Zeus. Originally there was only one Muse. Over time, they grew to number nine goddesses, suggesting an expansion of their powers. Each of the nine Muses concerned herself with an area of art. The power of the Muses still exists today, though mainly in our language. When we are amused, we are reminded of the charms wielded by these graceful goddesses.

Look at art that inspires you.

73

Mut

NURTURANCE

BIRTH

CREATION

Mut, whose name means "mother," was thought by the ancient Egyptians to help mothers give birth to children with sound bodies. She was honored as the mother of mothers, since it was believed that the cosmos sprang from her. This goddess was usually depicted as a vulture or in the form of a woman's body with a vulture head; Egyptians believed vultures bore the ability to reproduce without male involvement. As patroness of the city of Thebes, Mut was acknowledged as the consort of the god Amun.

For women who bear wounds from their maternal relationships, mother Mut invites us to find healing within ourself. While we cannot change the past, we are able to fulfill any needs that remain unresolved.

It is time to mother yourself. Healing awaits.

Nügua

CREATION

GOOD LUCK

HUMANITY

This ancient Chinese goddess was believed to bear the tail of a dragon. In Chinese tradition, dragons are considered very fortuitous and are associated with water, a universal symbol of wealth and fertility.

Because Nügua was the first deity to live upon the earth after it was created, she was lonely. To fill her time, the goddess mixed dirt and water, inventing a compound she named clay. The clay inspired Nügua to sculpt numerous small figures. By animating these small sculptures with her breath, she created the first humans. Due to this act, Nügua is honored as a creator of life.

Share your creativity with the world
to ease your isolation.

Nut

THE SKY
THE STARS
PROTECTION

Nut, whose name translates as "night," was a mother goddess worshiped by the ancient Egyptians as the physical personification of the night sky. Paintings depict her as a beautiful, naked woman covered in stars, her body sharply arched over the earth in protection. She was married to Geb, the god who represented the verdant earth.

One myth relates that the sun god, Ra, was reborn each morning from Nut's womb; the rosy color of the sunrise symbolized her blood as she pushed him out into the sky. It was also believed that the dead were taken into Nut's celestial vault, where the goddess would eternally protect and nurture them.

You are reborn from night each morning.
Start anew.

Nyai Loro Kidul

POWER

SEDUCTION

TRANSFORMATION

The royal family of the island of Java claim that their divine right to rule was bestowed on them by Nyai Loro Kidul, the mermaid goddess of the South Seas. One popular tale says that this goddess married the king of Java in the sixteenth century and taught him how to gain the power of the spirits, so he could rule Java wisely. Another story about her bears similarities to the fairy tale *Cinderella*. It tells how Nyai Loro Kidul was poisoned by a jealous stepmother. To cure herself, she threw herself into the sea, where she was transformed into a goddess.

Today, mortals fear falling victim to the goddess's seductive charms. It is believed that Nyai Loro Kidul seeks men to serve her in her undersea realm. Those who live to tell after encountering her speak of the mermaid goddess's undeniable power—a power as seductive as the fathomless sea.

Powerful forces lie within you. Do not avoid them.

Ogboinba

GODDESS OF PROPHECY

HEALING

THE FUTURE

DISCONTENT

Ogboinba was the daughter of Woyengi, the Nigerian mother goddess. Though Ogboinba possessed magical abilities that enabled her to heal the sick and predict the future, she was not content; Ogboinba yearned to become pregnant, a power she did not possess. Even though she passed through seven kingdoms and risked death to gain this ability, the goddess remained childless.

The story of Ogboinba reminds us of the power of contentment. Despite the many gifts the goddess possessed, she was unable to find happiness within herself. If we spend all our time seeking our desires, we neglect to appreciate all we have now.

Though it is good to desire,
sometimes it is better to possess contentment.

Oshun

WATER

LOVE

FERTILITY

The Yoruba goddess Oshun is as sparkling as the African river that bears her name. Oshun's beauty is intoxicating—her dark skin is as sleek as velvet, and her elaborate headdress is made of richly hued feathers that set off her brilliant eyes. Worshiped in both Africa and the Caribbean, flirtatious Oshun is a popular goddess for those wishing to attract love. The fertility of women, a product of love, falls under her many concerns as a water deity.

Though honored as the Modest One, Oshun nonetheless delights in adorning herself. To be desirable to her beloved, the goddess dresses herself with gleaming jewels, ornaments made of brass and yellow copper, and luxurious silks. Oshun is also associated with wealth. Some believe she wears seven bracelets upon her graceful arm, along with a mirror attached to her belt, to view her divine beauty.

To encourage love, find the beauty in yourself.

Oya

ELOQUENCE

STRENGTH

LEADERSHIP

The Yoruba people believe that the Niger River is ruled by a powerful goddess named Oya. Valued for her charming but penetrating language, many consider the goddess a patroness of feminine leadership; her gift for eloquence helps women speak with confidence and strength.

Oya is a goddess to be approached with great respect. In Nigeria, shrines to her are set into a corner of a home. The altars are often molded of packed earth. Arranged around it are magical amulets and objects. A sword represents Oya's power of incisive speech. Strings of red, orange, or brown glass beads, buffalo horns, and locust pods also symbolize the goddess. Finally, small dishes of her favorite foods, eggplant and *akara*, are offered to please Oya, goddess of the winds.

When the time is right, you will speak with authority.

Pajau Yan
LADY MOON

LUCK

HEALTH

CHANGES

In Vietnam, Pajau Yan is invoked as Lady Moon, a benevolent goddess who offers her worshipers health and good fortune. She is usually honored on the first day of the waning moon. It is also believed that lunar eclipses are her way of granting glory to the sun.

One story claims that Pajau Yan originally resided on the earth. She was sent to the moon to stop her from raising the dead back to life. This myth suggests that we cannot change that which has already taken place; all we can do is make peace with it. Nonetheless, Pajau Yan is able to share her goodwill with humanity from her celestial home.

No matter what changes may come,
you will be at peace.

Pele

VOLCANOES

PASSION

ANGER

The Hawaiians believe in a tempestuous goddess named Pele. Pele rules over all kinds of fire, but especially over lava that flows from erupting volcanoes. Famed for her love affairs as well as her temper, Pele often appears to her worshipers in the guise of a woman as beautiful as the moon. Others say she looks like a terrible hag, with brown flesh as crumpled as coarse lava. Whichever way the goddess chooses to present herself, all agree about her fiery temperament and her ability to destroy as well as create.

The passion of anger has an urgency that can help us better our lives. Pele's ability to present herself as either a wrinkled hag or a seductive woman suggests the inner turmoil that rage can create in women. It reveals the ugliness and discomfort that women often feel when angered—along with the empowerment that anger can bring.

Be empowered by anger.

Persephone
THE MAIDEN

THE SEASONS

SEXUALITY

INNOCENCE

Persephone, the treasured daughter of the harvest goddess Demeter, was honored by the ancient Greeks as the queen of the underworld. She is also acknowledged as the *kore* or maiden aspect of the triple goddess.

Persephone's transformational journey from maiden to queen of the underworld was instigated when Pluto, god of death, kidnapped her. The girl's heart was unmoved by the god's declarations of devotion. Instead, she wept for her mother and refused to eat. Finally, after some time had passed, Persephone tasted six seeds of the pomegranate. This act defined the goddess's life, for it symbolized Persephone's reluctant acceptance of her sexuality and of Pluto as her husband. It also ensured her separation from her mother, Demeter, for a month for each seed. This myth was used by the ancient Greeks to explain the creation of spring and winter.

Find ways to use your innocence as a strength.

Psyche
THE SOUL

LOVE

TRANSFORMATION

MATURATION

In classical Greece and Rome, the goddess Psyche began her life as a mortal woman whose unworldly beauty won her divinity and the love of a god more powerful than any. Cupid, the handsome son of Venus, fell in love with the girl when he viewed her sleeping one night. To be joined with Cupid, Psyche endured many tests of courage to prove her worth.

Psyche symbolizes the woman's soul as love transforms her from innocence to wisdom; the Greek word for both "butterfly" and "soul" is *psyche*. Psyche is often depicted with the translucent wings of a butterfly, suggesting her transformation from mortal girl to goddess. After the ultimate transformation of death, many traditions hold that the spirit leaves the body in the form of a butterfly or moth.

Allow love to transform your soul. You are ready for it.

Rati

PASSION

LOVE

PREGNANCY

Worshiped in India, beautiful Rati bears the ripe body of a heavily pregnant woman. Her passion-inspiring powers share similarities with Venus, the Roman goddess of love. Though Rati was daughter to the fiery sun god Daksha, she is associated with water. The Apsaras—a group of water goddesses as changeable as the tide—include this Hindu love goddess among their many members. Renowned for their bewitching, shapeshifting powers, the Apsaras often take on the appearance of seductive women who are impossible to resist.

Rati's passionate powers inspired a book similar to the *Kama Sutra*, entitled the *Ratirahasya*; the name of this book translates as "the secrets of love." The love goddess's secrets are exposed within its explicit pages, which include numerous techniques to bring lovers pleasure.

Embrace your passion.

Rhiannon

THE HORSE GODDESS

PROGRESS

HAPPY ENDINGS

DESIRE

In the *Mabinogion*, a collection of Welsh myths, the horse goddess Rhiannon is presented as an unattainable enchantress dressed in rich gold. Pwyll, the prince of Dyfed, fell in love with her after spying the ethereal beauty on her white horse. Pwyll guessed she was of divine origin, but he was undaunted. He rode his horse as fast as he could to catch up to her. But no matter how fast he rode, he was unable to reach the goddess.

Finally, the humbled prince called to Rhiannon to wait for him, which she did. When he asked, "Why didn't you stop earlier?" she simply replied, "Why didn't you ask me?" And so Rhiannon accepted Pwyll as her consort. The story of Rhiannon and Pwyll suggests that our desires are always within our reach. For them to be fulfilled, sometimes all we need to do is ask.

Choose an action to reach your goal. Now is the time.

Saci

PHYSICAL STRENGTH

LEADERSHIP

OBSERVATION

Also known as Indrani, Saci is the wife of Indra, the supreme ruling god during the Vedic period in early Hindu mythology. This goddess is renowned for her physical strength and is associated with the lion and the elephant, two animals of exceptional power. Some accounts claim she bears one thousand eyes in her beautiful face, perhaps signifying acute powers of observation.

Another tale claims Saci as a goddess of wrath and jealousy. This suggests the discomfort that some may have experienced when confronted with a strong female deity.

Take steps to develop your physical strength.

Sarasvati

WISDOM

EDUCATION

MUSIC

Sarasvati, the Hindu goddess of all knowledge, is held in special esteem in India by students, writers, and musicians. Extraordinarily beautiful and graceful, Sarasvati is easily recognizable by her dazzling white skin and brilliant clothing. One myth tells how Sarasvati and her consort, Brahma, were born from a golden egg that had emerged from the sea. They then created all of the knowledge and creatures of the world.

Sarasvati is able to banish all forms of ignorance, bringing education to anyone wise enough to desire her enlightening presence. Paintings depict her seated upon a lotus-blossom throne, accompanied by a white swan. The swan is believed to be able to separate milk from water—an act which shows the ability to discriminate between actions that are good and those that are insincere.

Enlightenment awaits you. Prepare for it.

Sekhmet

ENCHANTMENTS

STRENGTH

THE UNDERWORLD

This fearless Egyptian goddess is connected with the sun and depicted in the form of a lion or as a lion-headed woman. Sekhmet was renowned for her delight in violence, war, and hunting. Honored as the Mighty One, she ruled over strength, vengeance, and enchantments—forceful actions used to wield change in the world.

Sekhmet was also a goddess of the underworld, where she has a special connection to the art of mummification. Egyptians viewed mummification as a magical ritual that enabled the physical body to live forever. Perhaps to suggest this ability, Sekhmet was often presented with an ankh, a potent symbol of eternal life.

Let your darker emotions bring you strength.

Shakti

FEMININITY

SEXUALITY

LIFE FORCE

The goddess Shakti is honored in several ways in India. In Tantric tradition, Shakti is the powerful feminine counterbalance to masculine energy. In the Vedic religion, she is a goddess of sexuality and the beloved consort of Shiva, whom some consider the oldest named god known to humanity.

Shakti's name translates as "divine energy"—an appropriate honorific for a deity who animates all of life. This primordial deity is the personification of creative energy in motion, a goddess who empowers people toward action.

Be filled with divine energy.
Use it to move forward in your life.

Sophia

THE SOUL

KNOWLEDGE

PURITY

The goddess Sophia is considered the divine embodiment of feminine wisdom; her name translates literally as "wisdom" in Greek. In the ancient Near East, Sophia provided humans with the knowledge needed to create literature and the arts. Sophia symbolized the soul in its purest manifestation; she is often represented in art as having the form of a dove.

Later history associated Sophia with the Holy Spirit in Gnosticism. Gnosticism—derived from *gnosis*, the Greek word for "knowledge"— grew alongside early Christianity. Some gnostic traditions even claimed Sophia as the mother of Christ. An important tenet of Gnosticism held that knowledge could free humanity from the shackles of limitation; it enabled the divine spirit every person possessed to return to the unknowable source of creation.

Listen to the wisdom of your soul.

Spider Woman

GODDESS OF CREATION

CONNECTIONS

CREATION

DIVERSITY

Many cultures around the world believe that all of the world's creatures are connected by a strong but delicately woven web. The Pueblo Indians credit the spinning of this web of life to a goddess so potent that her true name is never spoken aloud. Some call this goddess Spider Woman.

Spider Woman existed before the world existed. By spinning and chanting, she was able to create the four directions of the universe. Within this sacred space, she produced her daughters, Ut Set and Nau Ut Set. Following their mother's directions, Ut Set and Nau Ut Set made the sun, moon, and stars. As she spun her web, Spider Woman made all of life, including the mountains, lakes, oceans, and deserts. She also created the different races of people from colored clays. Finally, using a last thread of her web, Spider Woman connected each human being to her.

Find a way to connect the threads.

Tara

COMPASSION

WISH FULFILLMENT

ASSISTANCE

Tibetan Buddhists believe that the goddess Tara has the power to heal all sorrows and grant all wishes. The name *Tara* translates into English as "she who causes one to cross," which means that the goddess will help her devotees cross to the other side of their difficulties.

Tara was believed to be a mortal woman who yearned to became the first female buddha. One story claims that to reach this goal, she prayed for the welfare of humans for over ten million years. Then she was transformed into a goddess whose only desire was to ease the world's pain.

Tara is often depicted with differently colored skins, suggesting her realms of influence. She is most popularly seen as White Tara and Green Tara. As White Tara, the goddess is renowned for her compassion. Green Tara is believed to grant wishes to her most loyal devotees.

Your wish can be granted if you ask for help.

Tlazolteotl

THE FILTH EATER

PURIFICATION

CARNALITY

MAGIC

Tlazolteotl was acknowledged in Aztec legend as a powerful goddess of sexuality as well as the patroness of midwives. Statues of Tlazolteotl depict her in the act of giving birth to the sun. This goddess's expansive realm envelops the deepest forms of carnality and the most intense forms of black magic.

Later, Tlazolteotl was thought to purify her followers upon their death by devouring their misdeeds after they had confessed them. In this function, the goddess was known as the Filth Eater and was honored for her valuable service to humanity.

Look within and be honest with yourself.
Then you will be freed.

Ukemochi

FECUNDITY

KINDNESS

SACRIFICE

The Japanese once believed that all the food of the earth was created by Ukemochi, a gentle and kind goddess. Because of Ukemochi's generosity, no one was ever short of food.

Upon her death, Ukemochi allowed her body to continue creating food and other items to help humans. Grain sprouted from her forehead; its seed blew into the meadows and grew into vast, fertile fields. Rice plants sprouted from the goddess's belly, to bring plenty to all. Her inky eyebrows became silkworms, whose threads were woven into rainbow-colored silks to clothe the gods and goddesses. Ukemochi's myth later became associated with the story of the Japanese rice deity, Inari.

Be generous to benefit another.
You have the means to do so.

Venus

PASSION

LOVE

SENSUALITY

Venus was the name the ancient Romans gave to the goddess of love. Created from the union of sea and sky, Venus was born of sea foam and water and brought to earth upon a conch shell. She was described as "the star of the sea" by her worshipers and considered the queen of pleasure. For hundreds of years, artists and poets have turned to her for inspiration.

Venus is the goddess who inspires people to love each other, ensuring that the human race continues to grow. She was known to the Greeks as Aphrodite; Aphrodite's name translates literally as "she who comes from the foam." Her attendants, three Graces named Joyous, Brilliance, and Flowering, illustrate the wonders the goddess can offer if she chooses to smile upon our earthly petitions.

Love will bring you pleasure.

Xochiquetzal

THE FLOWER GODDESS

HAPPINESS

THE ARTS

LOVE

The Aztecs, a people who ruled over a vast empire in Mexico during the Middle Ages, believed in a flower goddess whom they called Xochiquetzal. The goddess's sacred flower was the yellow marigold; her name meant "feather flower," referring to the marigold's many feathery petals. One of the happiest of the Aztec deities, Xochiquetzal was also the goddess of dance, music, crafts, and love. Appropriately, her twin brother, Xochipilli, was honored as the god of pleasure.

Xochiquetzal lived on top of a mountain above the nine heavens. This flower-laden garden was populated by merry dwarves, dancing maidens, and musicians. The Aztecs believed that anyone who was faithful to the goddess would spend eternity in her paradise when their life had ended.

Take time to appreciate all of life's joys.

Yemanja

FERTILITY

GRACE

THE OCEAN

Yemanja, the Santerian goddess of water, is the daughter of the earth goddess Oddudua and the sister and wife of the god Aganju. As the mother goddess of their pantheon, she occupies an exalted position in the Santerian religion.

Moon, sea, women—indeed, the eternal cycles of life—all fall under Yemanja's expansive domain. Since she is the powerful goddess of the waters, many honor the goddess with the title of Holy Queen Sea. She is said to rule over every sea creature, and she brings rain to nourish the earth. Since the ocean is analogous to the waters that nurture life within a woman's womb, Yemanja also reigns over fertility.

Surrender to the flow of life.
It will transport you to where you need to be.

Zhinu

WEAVING WOMAN OF HEAVEN

THE STARS

CREATIVITY

ORIGINALITY

The Chinese goddess Zhinu is the divine patroness of weaving. She is responsible for making the elaborately decorated robes worn by the Heavenly Emperor and his family and is similar to a fairy in her demeanor.

Zhinu is also associated with the heavens, whose movements are believed to weave fate. Some claim she resides within the constellation Lyra on Vega, a brilliant star. One story connects the creation of the Milky Way to this goddess. When Zhinu fell in love with a mortal herdsman, she began to neglect her weaving, much to the immortals' frustration. To keep the two lovers apart, the gods placed a river of stars between them. But a flock of magpies took pity: the birds flew together to form a bridge over the Milky Way, reuniting the goddess with her beloved.

Let the stars inspire you.

Find an original way to surmount an obstacle.

The Zorya

THE SUN

THE UNIVERSE

PROTECTION

In cultures all over the world, there have always been trinities of goddesses who bear responsibility for the earth's well-being. Usually these three goddesses symbolize the three stages of women—maiden, mother, and crone. The universal presence of these triple goddesses suggest the strength and authority of the Divine Feminine everywhere. In Russian folklore, the Zorya are such a trinity of goddesses.

The Zorya represent and are named after different times of the day. The first goddess is called Morning Star; the second Evening Star; and the third Midnight. As well as attending to the sun god, the Slavic goddesses Zorya are guardians of the universe. As such, the goddesses are responsible for guarding a terrible doomsday hound, which is chained to the constellation of Ursa Minor, or Little Bear.

Be at peace. The Divine Feminine watches over you.

Part Three

Additional Information

$\mathcal{M}$ost of the art featured in the *Goddess Inspiration Oracle* was created for the tenth-anniversary edition of *The Book of Goddesses: A Celebration of the Divine Feminine*, published by Abrams Books in 2006. Others appeared in earlier publications. These include *Sacred Animals*, *Persephone and the Pomegranate*, *The Lover's Path Tarot*, and the first edition of *The Book of Goddesses*. The sole exception is the painting for Gaia. It was painted specifically for this deck and is inspired by a drawing I made for *Embracing the Goddess Within: A Creative Guide for Women*.

While some of these goddess paintings were also reproduced in *The Goddess Tarot*, they are presented in the *Goddess Inspiration Oracle* in a different format. This is to emphasize the differing intentions of the *Goddess Inspiration Oracle*, which offers examples of the Divine Feminine outside the structure of a tarot deck. Though I love and have worked with tarot for over two decades, it does have very particular constraints that must be honored. That written, I am thankful that *The Goddess Tarot* has served to introduce many to goddess myths from around the globe.

The majority of the eighty paintings featured in this deck were created in watercolor. Gouache and pencil, both lead and color, were used for fine detail. These paintings were painted on Arches 90 lb. cold-pressed 100% cotton rag paper, which had been stretched onto a piece of wood for stability. An Epson archival ink-jet printer was used to transfer most of the paintings' preliminary sketches onto paper; these sketches were first scanned to create a digital file, thus preserving the energy of the original drawings.

With only a few exceptions, the goddesses are depicted in the form of a woman, with the clothing, jewelry, and demeanor appropriate to the culture in which they appear. I often enlisted friends and colleagues to pose who reminded me in some way of a particular goddess's characteristics. Sometimes the resemblance was physical. Other times, it was contained within their life story—for example, my model for Demeter was a woman who had recently given birth. Choosing models in this manner made the art more personal for me. It also reflected my belief that the sacred is human, the human sacred.

I also studied traditional representations of each goddess—paintings, sculptures, even Navajo sand paintings, as in the case of Changing Woman.

Many of my paintings incorporate traditional design motifs from the cultures in which these goddesses originated.

The art on the back of each card portrays a serene moon goddess. She is Everywoman, ageless and raceless. Her eyes look inward, suggesting the organic wisdom all women possess; the wings crowning each side of her head allow her thoughts to take flight toward higher matters.

My intention with these goddess paintings, especially the more recent ones, was to create a concentrated, jewellike medium in which to honor these sacred women. Many of these paintings are intended to look like a precious relic from a medieval or renaissance illuminated manuscript.

The graphic design for the *Goddess Inspiration Oracle* mirrors this intention though the use of gold decorative borders and ornamental papers. These cards are meant as precious, beautiful objects in which to access inspiration from the Divine Feminine.

SELECTED BIBLIOGRAPHY

$\mathcal{O}$ver the past decade, most of my creative work has centered around the Divine Feminine. This bibliography is drawn from the numerous books and publications I have consulted during this period. Included within it are my own goddess-oriented books and tarot decks.

For those of you who are just discovering goddesses, I highly recommend these three books to begin with. Margot Adler's *Drawing Down the Moon* was the first book I read that led me to the Divine Feminine. Though *Drawing Down the Moon* presents a scholarly survey of earth-based religions, it answered questions about goddesses that had simmered inside me for years, recasting the world in a new light. Though the next two books were consulted later in my search, I can write similar praise about Merlin Stone's *When God Was a Woman* and Barbara Walker's *The Woman's Encyclopedia of Myths and Secrets.* They have also influenced my work and the way I perceive the world.

The remainder of the books in this list are treasures to anyone interested in the Divine Feminine. I hope they will aid you in your journey.

Adler, Margot. *Drawing Down the Moon*. Beacon, 1986.

Ann, Martha, and Dorothy Myers Imel. *Goddesses in World Mythology*. Oxford University Press, 1993.

Baring, Anne, and Jules Cashford. *The Myth of the Goddess*. Viking Books, 1992.

Bell, Robert E. *Women of Classical Mythology: A Biographical Dictionary*. Oxford University Press, 1993.

Bolen, Jean Shinoda. *Goddesses in Everywoman: A New Psychology of Women*. HarperCollins, 1985.

———. *Goddesses in Older Women: Archetypes in Women Over Fifty*. HarperCollins, 2001.

Bulfinch, Thomas. *Bulfinch's Mythology*. Signet/New American Library, 1962.

Campbell, Joseph. *The Masks of God: Primitive Mythology*. Arkana/Penguin USA, 1987.

Carmody, Denise Lardner. *Mythological Woman: Contemporary Reflections on Ancient Religious Stories*. Crossroad Publishing Company, 1992.

Davidson, H. R. Ellis. *Myths and Symbols in Pagan Europe: Early Scandinavian and Celtic Religions*. Syracuse University Press, 1988.

Downing, Christine, editor. *The Long Journey Home: Re-visioning the Myth of Demeter and Persephone for Our Time*. Shambhala, 1994.

Frazer, Sir James G. *The Golden Bough: A Study in Magic and Religion*. The MacMillan Company, 1958.

Gadon, Elinor W. *The Once and Future Goddess*. Harper and Row, 1989.

Gimbutas, Marija. *The Goddesses and Gods of Old Europe, 6500-3500 B.C. Myths and Cult Images*. University of California Press, 1982.

Grimal, Pierre, editor. *Larousse World Mythology*. Hamlyn Publishing Group, 1968.

Harding, M. Esther. *Woman's Mysteries: Ancient and Modern*. Harper Perennial Library, 1976.

Kraemer, Ross Shepard. *Her Share of the Blessings: Woman's Religions Among Pagans, Jews, and Christians in the Greco-Roman World*. Oxford University Press, 1992.

Larrington, Carolyne, editor. *The Feminist Companion to Mythology*. Pandora/HarperCollins, 1992.

Monaghan, Patricia. *The Book of Goddesses and Heroines*. Llewellyn Publications, 1993.

Nicholson, Shirley. *The Goddess Re-awakening*. Quest Books, 1989.

Sered, Susan Starr. *Priestess, Mother, Sacred Sister: Religions Dominated by Women*. Oxford University Press, 1994.

Spretnak, Charlene. *Lost Goddesses of Early Greece*. Beacon Press, 1992.

Starhawk. *The Spiral Dance*. HarperCollins, 1979.

Stone, Merlin. *Ancient Mirrors of Womanhood*. Beacon Press, 1991.

———. *When God Was a Woman*. Harvest/Harcourt Brace Jovanovich Books, 1976.

Sykes, Egerton. *Who's Who in Non-Classical Mythology*. Oxford University Press, 1993.

Waldherr, Kris. *The Book of Goddesses: A Celebration of the Divine Feminine*. Abrams Books, 2006.

———. *The Lover's Path Tarot*. US Games Systems, 2004.

———. *Sacred Animals*. HarperCollins Books, 2001.

———. *The Goddess Tarot*. US Games Systems, 1998.

———. *Embracing the Goddess Within: A Creative Guide for Women*. Beyond Words Publishing, 1997.

———. *The Book of Goddesses*. Beyond Words Publishing, 1996.

———. *Persephone and the Pomegranate*. Dial Books/Penguin USA, 1993.

Walker, Barbara G. *The Women's Encyclopedia of Myths and Secrets*. HarperSanFrancisco, 1983.

$\mathcal{T}$he illustrated publications of author, illustrator, and designer Kris Waldherr are well known to lovers of mythology and goddesses. They include *The Lover's Path Tarot*, *Sacred Animals*, and *The Book of Goddesses*. *The Book of Goddesses* inspired a music CD, several illustrated calendars, and *The Goddess Tarot*. Waldherr's picture-book retelling of the Persephone myth, *Persephone and the Pomegranate*, was praised by the *New York Times Book Review* for its "quality of myth and magic," and by Jean Shinoda Bolen, M.D., author of the *Goddesses in Everywoman*, as "a beautifully done retelling of the major mother-daughter myth."

Waldherr recently published her first illustrated novel, *The Lover's Path*, which was praised as "a visual adventure" by Women in the Arts. She has also had illustrations published as greeting cards, book covers, and in magazines. Her artwork has been shown in galleries and museums throughout the United States, including the National Museum of Women in the Arts. She received her BFA at the School of Visual Arts.

Kris Waldherr lives and works in Brooklyn with her husband, anthropologist Thomas Ross Miller, and their daughter, Thea. To learn more about Waldherr's art and publications, visit www.artandwords.com and her online gallery at www.kriswaldherr.com.

Visit the *Goddess Inspiration Oracle* online at
www.goddessinspiration.net.